D0542497

Arnaud Chicurel would like to thank the following people:

Anita Garcia, Lionel Lourdel, and Bela Chicurel for their constant support.
Franck Lacombe for his participation in preparing the texts.
Émeric Fisset of Les Éditions Transboréal for his friendly and sage advice.

Pascal Ducept would like to thank the following people and organizations:

My parents for their unwavering support in the past few years.
Captain Xavier Tabbagh, Curator of the Army's Health Service Museum at Val-de-Grâce, and the Paris Police Prefecture communications service.
The Novotel Paris Les Halles and specially Renata Ramos.
Emmanuel Baumgartner (Cabinet Baumgartner) and Christophe Léman.

© 2011 Parigramme / Compagnie Parisienne du Livre (Paris)

MONUMENTS OF PARIS

THE SPLENDORS OF THE CITY OF LIGHT

PHOTOGRAPHS
Arnaud Chicurel
Pascal Ducept

English translation by
Lilith Cowan

PARIGRAMME

Although we know that you can't reduce cities to their monuments, we can surely agree that they are enhanced by them.

Paris is quite well served in this regard, with palaces, great museums, prestigious squares, arches, and churches – so many landmarks dotted along the Seine and elsewhere… It's no surprise that great monuments make an impression; that's what they're there for! Their size, decoration, and shape set them apart from ordinary buildings and make them extraordinary places marked for special visits. Plus, unlike run-of-the-mill constructions which don't have anything to tell us, monuments generally speak volumes, celebrating the glory of God or of a sovereign, the vitality of a nation, or its faith in the future… History sometimes contradicts these manifestoes but nonetheless imbues the structures with meaning, memories, and images by using them as its theater. We heard the bells of Notre-Dame during the Liberation of Paris. We saw the Vendôme column dashed to the cobblestones during the Paris Commune. We measured the vanity of human undertakings when Napoleon's ashes were returned under the Arc de Triomphe…

However, there is also a more mundane, more practical aspect to great monuments. They are landmarks known to all and, ultimately, the basis for our shared urban language. We realize this when we make sure to specify "I live at Madeleine"; of course, no one's going to think that you live in a sacristy! Naturally, we resort to the medieval habit of using remarkable buildings to orient ourselves; in medieval times, street names weren't clearly defined or numbered.

Beyond their specific histories, the reasons for which they came to be, Parisian monuments which have withstood the test of time have become communal property and are there for anyone who cares to seek them out.

That's what photographers Arnaud Chicurel and Pascal Ducept did. For more than three years, they constantly looked for original points of view, watched the skies, clambered onto makeshift perches, and took advantage of digital techniques so their images could breathe an extra measure of life into Paris' architectural heritage. As they photographed the capital's monuments, they created a close relationship with them and with their builders' creative thoughts.

Pont-Neuf

Between Quai de la Mégisserie (1st) and Quai des Grands-Augustins (6th)

Created by Henry III to make the traffic flow more smoothly through the Île de la Cité, the Pont-Neuf was inaugurated in 1607 by Henry IV, who gave it its name. For the king, this construction was part of a vast urban-planning operation that also included the creation of Place Dauphine and the street of the same name.
The Pont-Neuf was immediately a great success. The first stone bridge without houses, it provided a new view of the Seine. At 28 meters wide, which was exceptional at the time, the Pont-Neuf had sidewalks and recessed half-circles protecting pedestrians from passing carriages and horses. Parisians flocked there in droves to stroll, dawdling to watch street performers or inspect itinerant salesmen's wares. The capital's oldest bridge honors the memory of Henry IV, whose equestrian statue stands upon it.

Conciergerie

1, Quai de l'Horloge (1st)

The medieval silhouette of the Conciergerie on the banks of the Seine is part of a prestigious setting that is both alluring and picturesque. This is where the French kings' palaces stood until the end of the 14th century, when sovereigns began to favor the residences of the Hôtel Saint-Pol or the Louvre. The palace then became the seat of parliament and the judicial center of the capital.
The Conciergerie was the prison of the royal palace of La Cité, built in 1298 by Philip the Fair, and remained the largest prison in Paris until the end of the 19th century. Its name came from the royal steward, known as the "concierge", who received fees from the shops set up around the palace walls. He also charged rent for the cells and their meager furniture!
This is where Queen Marie-Antoinette, among many others, was held in 1793 before she was tried by the Revolutionary Court and sentenced to death.
In 1914, the Conciergerie became an historical museum where you can visit the Guard Room and the rib-vaulted Hall of Men at Arms dating from the early 14th century, the prisoners' hallway, the queen's expiatory chapel, and the reconstruction of her cell.

Île Saint-Louis

(4th arrondissement)

If you're looking for a village in the heart of Paris, you'll find one on the Île Saint-Louis. Here, amblers don't have any avenues to cross and won't see any Métro stations. There aren't any famous monuments, either, but the whole island is a monument in itself. Born in the 17th century from the combination of the inhabited islets of Notre Dame and Aux Vaches, it became the focus of a building operation, primarily for noble residents, which is why there is such a remarkable concentration of town houses. The most beautiful among them were built facing the river, for the view. They differ from the traditional Parisian town house "between courtyard and garden" because of the small lots. Less ornately decorated on the outside than, for example, the residences of the Marais, the town houses of the Île Saint-Louis featured sumptuous interior decoration. Some survive, like the long gallery of the Hôtel Lambert or the reception rooms of the Hôtel de Lauzun; in this last, the poet Baudelaire briefly rented a few rooms.

Sainte-Chapelle

4, Boulevard du Palais (1st)

The Sainte-Chapelle is the oldest vestige of the palace of La Cité, the French royal residence until the mid-14th century. Within the very walls of the palace, Saint Louis had a chapel built to house the relics of the Passion of Christ recently purchased from the Emperor of Constantinople.
The structure, an architectural transposition of a golden reliquary, was consecrated in 1248. It encountered various vicissitudes throughout its history. The renewed interest in the Gothic style in the early 19th century paved the way for the restoration of the Sainte-Chapelle in the 1840s, as well as the reconstruction of its spire, which had been torn down during the Revolution.
This tall, graceful monument is made up of two chapels, one on top of the other. The upper chapel was reserved for the royal family. Pierced with fifteen windows over 15 meters high, the upper part seems as much composed of stained glass as stone, a miracle of balance and lightness. The relics, once kept under the architectonic canopy, part of which is original, are now kept in the treasury of Notre-Dame de Paris.

Notre-Dame de Paris

Parvis Notre-Dame (4th)

Construction on Notre-Dame began in 1163 at the tip of the Île de la Cité, on the initiative of Bishop Maurice de Sully, and it was largely completed 90 years later. It's one of the oldest Gothic cathedrals and one of the last big churches with galleries. While it retains elements characteristic of early Gothic, the cathedral underwent a succession of major transformations: Louis XIII's wish to devote his kingdom to the Virgin if she gave him a son led to the destruction of the rood screen and the high altar. In the 18th century, the old stained-glass windows in the choir were removed and the trumeau of the central portal was destroyed. During the Revolution, the cathedral was used as a warehouse, and the figures of the kings of Judah on the façade were destroyed; they were mistaken for the kings of France. When Napoleon restored it for worship in 1802, the monument had been badly damaged. Victor Hugo's novel, *Notre-Dame de Paris* (1831), swayed popular opinion in favor of its restoration. The architects Lassus and especially Viollet-le-Duc undertook the task starting in 1844. Viollet-le-Duc proved an able and fine restorer, giving the cathedral back its sculpted decorations… and even adding a few pieces of his own design!

Haussmann's radical reorganization of the Île de la Cité got rid of the tangle of houses which surrounded Notre-Dame. Clearing the huge square we know today changed perceptions of the cathedral, which had been visible from great distances but could only be seen up close at the last minute, walking out of an alleyway.

The "parish of the history of France", Notre-Dame was nonetheless never the great sanctuary of the monarchy, as kings were crowned in Reims and interred in Saint-Denis Basilica.

Arc de Triomphe

Place Charles-de-Gaulle (8th)

"You shall not return to your homes," Napoleon declared to his troops after the victory at Austerlitz in 1805, "unless it's through triumphal arches." This one wasn't finished until 1836, twenty-one years after the end of the First Empire. This monument to the glory of the Great Army was adopted by the Republic: a huge French flag is raised on it during major national holidays and official celebrations at the site. Since 1921, the remains of the Unknown Soldier, fallen for France during the First World War, have rested beneath the arch. Above the grave, the Memorial Flame is rekindled every day. Because the tomb prevents parades from marching between the pillars, the arch is now a sanctuary.
This altar to the nation is imposing in the simplicity of its lines and it gigantic size; at 50 meters high, the Arc de Triomphe is the record-holder in its category. Its sculpted decoration, one of the most important such works of the 19th century, includes the notable "Le Départ des Volontaires" (The Volunteers' Departure) of 1792, a work by François Rude. It is more commonly referred to as "La Marseillaise".

Palais de Chaillot

Place du Trocadéro-et-du-11-Novembre (16th)

The Palais de Chaillot was built in 1937 for the last Universal Exhibition held in Paris. On its site stood the Palace of Trocadéro, built for the 1878 Exhibition and composed of a rotunda flanked by two minaret-like towers, to which were attached two curved wings. As time was of the essence and the ground was unstable, riddled with quarries, there was no option but to keep to the foundations already laid out for the first palace, and the architects cleverly clad the existing structure and maintained the curved wings. Their most revolutionary idea was certainly removing the central rotunda and towers and leaving the space… empty! How could the building compete with the Eiffel Tower, just across the way? By choosing to create a vast square, the architects provided not only an exceptional panoramic viewpoint on the Seine but managed to integrate the "iron lady" into their own composition.
The Palais de Chaillot holds a theater and several museums, including the "Cité de l'architecture et du patrimoine" (architecture and heritage museum), which features spectacular casts of major elements of French heritage and offers a wide variety of contemporary international creations.

Stairway at the Cité de l'Architecture et du Patrimoine.

Cast of the "Well of Moses" from the Chartreuse de Champmol in the Cast Gallery.

Grand Palais

Avenue Winston-Churchill (8th)

The Grand Palais was built between 1897 and 1900 for the Universal Exhibition. This gigantic metal structure has colonnaded stone façades on Avenue Winston Churchill and Avenue Franklin Roosevelt. The most spectacular space in the building is its great nave capped with a vast glass roof, itself crowned with a dome. Inside, a remarkable cast-iron staircase spreads its Art Nouveau volutes up to the gallery.
The structure holds the Palais de la Découverte (science museum) and is used for major art exhibitions.
The nave was used for many events – trade fairs for automobiles, housewares, books… – before being closed to the public in 1993 and undergoing major renovations until 2007, to fix problems with the roof. The structure was repaired, shored up, and the glass was completely replaced with modern, stronger, more resistant panes.

Place de la Concorde

(8th arrondissement)

The largest and certainly the most beautiful square in Paris, Place de la Concorde was created in the 18th century outside the city to showcase an equestrian statue of Louis XV. At the king's request, Jacques-Ange Gabriel designed a vast quadrilateral with cut corners, bordered by walkways. To the north and to the north alone, because the idea was to preserve the view along the Champs-Élysées and the view of the Seine, the architect built two palaces echoing the colonnades of the Louvre.
Dubbed Place Louis XV, the last Parisian royal square became Place de la Révolution in 1792 and was the site of more than one thousand public executions, including those of Louis XVI, Marie-Antoinette and, not long thereafter, Robespierre.
After several name changes, the square was finally named Concorde in 1830 when the July Monarchy, eager to make people forget the rifts of the Revolution, worked to alter the look of the square to make it as neutral as possible. The Luxor Obelisk, a gift from Egypt, was perfect for this purpose and was erected in the center of the square. New urban furniture – fountains, rostral columns, statues of French cities – were put in place by Hittorff between 1830 and 1844.

Madeleine Church

Place de la Madeleine (8th)

Nearly 80 years passed between the first stone's being laid for the Church of Saint-Marie de la Madeleine and its consecration in 1845. In the meantime, the structure changed shape several times. In the mid-18th century, in response to the growth of a neighborhood which then only had a modest parish at the start of the current Boulevard Malesherbes, it was decided to build a new, larger church. However, the proximity to Place de la Concorde, which was being designed at the time, gave the church an additional function: it was to complete the monumental ensemble of the square by standing at the end of the perspective of the Rue Royale.
The church was to have been capped by a dome similar to that on the Panthéon de Paris, built at the same time, but the Revolution interrupted construction and uses other than religious ones were found for the future building. Napoleon finally decided to make it a temple to the glory of the Great Army and gave it the appearance we know today. Under the Restoration, the building was finally devoted to Catholic worship, although its architecture evokes a Greco-Roman temple. The Madeleine is now the third most-visited church in Paris and has become the site of many great artists' funerals.

Place Vendôme

(1st arrondissement)

Created at the same time as the Place des Victoires, Place Vendôme was also dedicated to Louis XIV. There was even talk of linking them with a new street, but the project was scuttled for financial reasons. The wish to create a pendant in western Paris for the Place Royale – which wasn't yet Place des Vosges – moved Minister Louvois to start construction. As was the case for its sister in eastern Paris, the lots on the Place Vendôme were granted to private individuals who were under obligation to build the façades following the model designed by Jules Hardouin-Mansart. Furthermore, State administrations and services were to be assembled around a bronze royal statue.

However, an economic crisis turned the program into a speculative real-estate operation which only granted lots to luxury town houses. They were in keeping with the ideal of sober classicism in vogue at the time and fanned around an octagonal "place". In the center, the equestrian statue of Louis XIV as a Roman emperor was in harmony with the proportions of the buildings. It was melted down during the Revolution, the fate reserved for royal statues. The 44-meter-high column which replaced it changed the scale of the square.

Napoleon erected it in 1806 to celebrate the victory at Austerlitz. A replica of Trajan's Column in Rome, it is plated in bronze from enemy cannons. It supports a statue of the Emperor of the French dressed like Caesar.
Another major change in perspectives, this one lower to the ground, resulted from the opening of Rue de Castiglione and Rue de la Paix, which Napoleon wanted to link Rue de Rivoli to the "grands boulevards". Today, the prestigious Place Vendôme houses the biggest names in fine jewelry.

CHOREGRAPHIE
ACADEMIE NATIONALE DE MUSIQUE

Palais Garnier

Place de l'Opéra (9th)

It was after a failed attack against Napoleon III near the old opera house on Rue Le Peletier that a plan was formed to build a more secure new opera house. The construction of a new building was undertaken alongside a vast urban-planning operation aimed at renovating a whole neighborhood and cutting Avenue de l'Opéra through from the Palais Royal. The whole plan was part of the beautification of Paris, completely changing the face of the capital.

A competition in December 1860 selected the project by Charles Garnier, then a young unknown architect. For fifteen years, he invested himself fully in his work and supervised the most minute details. Before building could begin, however, he had to start by drying up the ground water…

This was not unconnected to the legend of the lake under the Opera, which was to have a bright future.

The building has a profusion of decoration, an abundance of polychrome marble, gilding, mosaics, statues… Its unabashed eclecticism juxtaposes references and juggles styles. When asked "What is it, exactly?" Garnier responded that his work marked the birth of the Napoleon III style!

Inside, the grand staircase, a veritable "monument within the monument", winds majestically, offering viewpoints, arcades, and balconies from which to see or be seen. The foyer brings to mind the Hall of Mirrors in Versailles, and the red and gold performance hall is ringed with five levels of boxes. Its original roof has been hidden since 1964 by Chagall's painting evoking famous operas. The great chandelier weighs more than six tons; it was designed by Charles Garnier.
The opera stages approximately two hundred performances a year, mainly ballets.

Palais-Royal

Between Rue de Valois
and Rue de Montpensier (1st)

Before being royal, this palace was cardinal. Mere steps from the Louvre, home to the king and the court, the Duke of Richelieu, principal minister and man of the church, bought up houses and lots in order to build a sumptuous palace on the site. Its garden would be the greatest in Paris at that time.
Richelieu promised that, upon his death, the palace would go to the king. That's what happened in 1642, and the palace – now royal – welcomed Anne of Austria and her son, the future King Louis XIV. Later, the king's brother, the Duke of Orléans, received the palace; it remained in the family's possession until the mid-19th century. In the meantime, the property underwent such great changes that there remains almost no trace of the Palais-Cardinal, except for the "Galerie des Proues" that runs along one side of the main courtyard, and a balcony at 6 Rue de Valois. Less than ten years after the Revolution, Philippe of Orléans, deeply in debt, thought of making residence buildings around the gardens and opening shops and galleries on the ground floor. The operation was a great success, and the site became one of the liveliest places in Paris.

Gaming and brothels flourished with abandon, because the police weren't allowed on the land. On July 12, 1789, it's here that the call to arms was launched for the Revolution. Under the Empire, cafés and restaurants continued to prosper… just like the site's amorous and libertine reputation. The party ended with the return of Louis Philippe, Duke of Orléans, to France. He reclaimed the family palace and ordered major renovations between 1815 and 1830. The property was confiscated in 1854 by Napoleon III, damaged during the Commune, and then restored. The Council of State and the Culture Ministry are housed there. In 1986, Daniel Buren installed truncated black and white columns in the main courtyard; this caused quite a stir.

Arc du Carrousel du Louvre

Place du Carrousel (1st)

This arch, less imposing that its big brother on the Place de l'Étoile, was also commissioned by Napoleon.
It was built between 1806 and 1808 by Percier and Fontaine, the great architects of the Empire.
Its walls are decorated with narrative bas-reliefs, and the red marble columns support stone soldiers. These figures represent the diverse corps of the imperial army rather than heroic figures, who would have had to be depicted nude, according to the then very fashionable cannons of theatrical antiquity.
The Arc du Carrousel acted as the formal gateway to the Tuileries Palace, which was destroyed in 1871, in the fire of the Commune. Since the palace disappeared, the monument has come to be the first landmark of the great historical axis of Paris, continued farther along by the arches that stand on Place de l'Étoile and La Défense district.

Louvre Museum

Rue de Rivoli (1st)

A royal palace turned temple of the arts, the Louvre started out as an austere medieval fortress. In the 16th century, Francis I had the fortifications razed and began to turn the château into a Renaissance palace. The work was continued by Henry IV who, in 1610, completed the long gallery along the Seine, linking the Louvre to the Tuileries Palace. Louis XIV decided to enlarge the Cour Carrée and surround it with new wings. He also commissioned the grand colonnade, a monumental entrance in keeping with the scale of the palace. Nevertheless, the king left many works incomplete, and the transfer of the court to the new Palace of Versailles meant the Louvre was left to the artists and the few opportunists who occupied it. The Revolution turned the palace into a museum composed of the royal collections. Napoleon began construction on the north wing (along the Rue de Rivoli), and his nephew Napoleon III finished it. Thus, he completed the "grand design" put forward by Henry IV nearly three centuries earlier, completely linking the Louvre to the Tuileries. The satisfaction was short-lived, because a few years later the Tuileries Palace fell victim to the fire of the Commune.

The Athena Mattei statue
in the Ancient Greek collection.

The Cour Marly.

President François Mitterrand's Grand Louvre project was completed in 1993. It freed up new spaces to present works of art in the world's largest museum by transferring the Finance Ministry from the Richelieu wing of the Louvre to Bercy in eastern Paris and by making new spaces underground. The glass pyramid designed by Ieoh Ming Pei is the main entrance to the museum. It gives light and volume to the foyer and also became the starting point for the royal axis marked out by the Arc du Carrousel and the Arc de Triomphe, as well as the Arch of La Défense, which was also inaugurated in 1989.

Les Halles

Between Rue Berger, Rue Pierre-Lescot, and Rue Rambuteau (1st)

The Forum des Halles was built on the site of the old Halles de Paris. These markets were transferred to Rungis in 1969. Despite protests, the iron pavilions designed by Baltard in the mid-19th century were razed and replaced by a vast shopping mall built above the largest underground train station in Paris, a hub for three regional train lines and several Métro lines.
A very busy spot in the heart of Paris, the Forum was inaugurated in 1979, but its architecture never appealed.
A massive renovation has been decided; it should change the face of the neighborhood by 2016.
The Innocents' Fountain, finely sculpted by Jean Goujon in the mid-16th century, stood at the corner of Rue Saint-Denis and Rue Berger. More than a fountain, it was a loggia from which neighborhood dignitaries could watch the parade of royal arrivals in Paris. When the Church of the Innocents against which it stood was demolished in 1788, it was moved to the center of the market which replaced the cemetery. With the construction of Baltard's new Halles, the fountain was moved once again. It shifted another few meters when the Forum des Halles was built.

Saint-Eustache Church

Place René-Cassin (1st)

If it weren't for the lack of towers and a forecourt, Saint-Eustache would have the proportions of a cathedral – it has the tallest nave of all the churches in Paris. Even more remarkably, this building, constructed between 1532 and 1637, features a Renaissance decor in a soaring Gothic structure. In the mid-17th century, its forest of flying buttresses astonished people, as did the flamboyant Gothic interior, with its ribbed vaults and their long pendant keystones. Nonetheless, the church borrows from the stylistic repertory of the Renaissance, as evidenced by the classical pillars, the semicircular arches, and the choir's stained-glass windows. The façade of Saint-Eustache was rebuilt in the classical style in the mid-18th century.

The working-class parish of the large Halles market, the church was also linked to royal power. The Louvre is nearby. Louis XIV had his first communion here, and Colbert, his controller, is buried here. Saint-Eustache boasts rare 17th-century Baroque frescoes as well as a real musical tradition. Liszt and Berlioz performed new works here and the organ rivals the one in Notre-Dame. The "cathedral of the Halles" is the neighborhood's main monument, along with the Bourse du Commerce (Commodities Exchange), which was the Halle au Blé (wheat market) in the 18th century. The roundness and regularity of its lines seem to balance the volume and the architectural ebullience of Saint Eustache.

BUS

Place des Victoires

(1st and 2nd arrondissement)

Built on the model of the royal square, with a statue of the sovereign in the middle of a relatively small space, Place des Victoires is different in a few ways. It wasn't commissioned by the king or an official institution but by a private individual, Marshal de la Feuillade, a member of Louis XIV's court. Furthermore, the initial sculpture was not an equestrian but a standing figure, and it seemed out of proportion with the neighboring houses. Finally, the streets didn't stretch from opposite sides of the square, so the effigy was always set against a built-up background. Alas, everything has changed!

The statue of Louis XIV was knocked down and melted during the Revolution. It wasn't until 1822 that Louis XIV reclaimed the square which had been created for him. Now, the king is on horseback, dressed as a Roman emperor but wearing a wig. Also, the architectural balance designed by Jules Hardouin-Mansart was disrupted in the 19th century. The buildings were raised up, some streets were widened, and Rue Étienne Marcel was cut, gutting one whole side of the square. Place des Victoires' layout remains exceptional, but it no longer acts as a backdrop for a royal likeness.

Hôtel de Ville (City Hall)

Place de l'Hôtel-de-Ville (4th)

A genuine palace, bigger than the Élysée and a rival to the Louvre of the kings, the scale of the Hôtel de Ville is in keeping with the power of the municipality of Paris, which has sometimes acted as a counter-power to the State. The clout of Paris and the executive's distrust thereof led to its being deprived of a mayor for over a century. It was only in 1975 that the status of the City was reformed. Two years later, Jacques Chirac was elected mayor, succeeding – in a manner of speaking – Jules Ferry, the mayor from 1870-1871.
The current Hôtel de Ville, completed in 1882, replaced the preceding building, constructed in the 16th century and burned during the Commune of 1871. It is a slightly larger replica, still in the Renaissance style, with a profusion of arcades, niches, mullioned windows, and sloped roofs. The host of statues lining the façades – famous Parisians and allegorical figures – makes the Hôtel de Ville a sanctuary for a collective memory.
The interior decoration is extremely rich; the great reception rooms are covered in gilt, sculpted stucco, and academic frescoes. The Salle des Fêtes (reception hall) is more than 50 meters long; the center of the ceilings are decorated with a composition by Benjamin Constant "La Ville de Paris conviant le monde à ses fêtes" (the city of Paris inviting the world to its celebrations).

The Galerie Galland.

The Salle des Fêtes.

Hôtel de Ville seen from Saint-Jacques Tower.

Saint-Jacques Tower

Square de la Tour-Saint-Jacques, between Rue de Rivoli and Avenue Victoria (4th)

The Tower is the last remnant of the church of Saint-Jacques de la Boucherie, which became national property during the Revolution, only to be destroyed shortly thereafter. Miraculously saved, Saint-Jacques Tower has a Gothic appearance despite its having been built, like the church for which it was the bell tower, at the beginning of the 16th century. Thousands of pilgrims started out from this point on the long road leading to Santiago de Compostela.

At ground level, a statue of Blaise Pascal reminds us that the scholar is said to have carried out experiments on the weight of air here in the mid-17th century. After the Revolution, Saint-Jacques Tower continued to test the laws of physics, because a lead-shot factory came up with the idea of using an original process there. From the top of the tower, the molten metal was dropped through conduits, breaking into shot and cooling as it fell.

The houses clustered around the foot of the Tower were cleared away when Rue de Rivoli and Boulevard de Sébastopol were cut. The Tower underwent major renovation in the mid-19th century. The statue of Saint-Jacques in particular, knocked down during the Revolution, was replaced.

Since 1891, the Tower has housed a small weather station; it is now one of the Airparif stations which measure air-pollution levels in Paris.

"L'ART DOIT DISCUTER,
DOIT CONTESTER,
DOIT PROTESTER"

Pompidou Center

Place Georges-Pompidou (4th)

This is without a doubt the monument which elicited the most passionate reactions and debate since… the construction of the Eiffel Tower, nearly a century earlier! "Refinery" to some, avant-garde creation to others, the Pompidou Center didn't leave anyone indifferent when it was built in the heart of Old Paris.

The initiative for this building came from President Georges Pompidou in 1969. He wanted to give Paris a worthy contemporary art center.

A jury selected the provocative project by young architects Piano and Rogers. The president did not approve but did not interfere.

Putting the load-bearing structure on the outside, the architects decided to free the Center's six floors of all walls and pillars. Similarly, pipes and technical conduits weren't concealed but rather put on show on Rue du Renard. The big tubes were different bright colors depending on whether they carried air, water, or electricity.

The main façade, which is 166 meters long, features a ziz-zagged escalator housed in a cylindrical structure, echoing the tubular theme.

Inaugurated in 1977, the building was dubbed "post-industrial" because of its explicit references to factory architecture, but oddly, it did not spawn any similar projects. Its main virtues are that it definitely spurred a general overhaul of museums and managed to draw five times as many visitors as had been expected.

Marais District

(3th and 4th arrondissements)

The Marais owes its name to the market gardens that had existed since the Middle Ages in this fertile area between the Seine and the site of today's "grands boulevards", which approximately follow the prehistoric curve of the river.
From the 12th century, many convents and abbeys set up in the Marais, starting with the Temple priory which cut vast plots of land into lots, cultivated others, and created new streets which still exist today.
In the 14th and 15th centuries, the neighborhood boasted two royal residences, the Hôtel Saint-Pol and the Hôtel des Tournelles, both now gone.
The golden age of the Marais came a bit later. It was the creation of the Place des Vosges by Henry IV in the early 17th century which sparked construction fever. The monks sold their land or built on the vast plots they owned, and the fields gave way to sumptuous town houses.
The district – especially to the north – was fashionable, sought after by noblemen and the very wealthy.
It remained so until the early 18th century. The Revolution led to the vast town houses being abandoned, pillaged, divided up, and transformed throughout the 19th century, housing all sorts of workshops and industrial activities. Once aristocratic, the district became disadvantaged until the massive salvage plan passed in 1962 (the Malraux law), which began the renovation.
Now, this historic district has the highest concentration of town houses anywhere in Paris.

The **Hôtel Carnavalet**, built in the mid-16th century, was enlarged and remodeled by François Mansart in 1660. The stately home remains connected to the memory of Madame de Sévigné, who resided there for the twenty years before her death. It now houses the rich collections of the lovely historical museum of the City of Paris.
23, Rue de Sévigné (3rd)

LOUIS XIV

The **Hôtel de Sens** is a rare Parisian example of secular architecture from the Middle Ages. It was built by Tristan Salazar, Bishop of Sens, in the late 15th and early 16th century. The stately home didn't house only clerics, because the famous and tempestuous Queen Margot, ex-wife of Henry IV, lived there in 1605. Several craft workshops succeeded each other in the building over the course of the 19th century before it was purchased in 1911, practically in ruins, by the City. Restored, and with many parts fairly freely rebuilt, the Hôtel de Sens now houses the Forney library.

1, Rue du Figuier (4th)

The **Hôtel de Soubise** resulted from the early 18th-century transformation of a former medieval town house whose door is still visible at 58, Rue des Archives. For François de Rohan, Prince of Soubise, the architect Delamair created a spectacular main courtyard on the site of the former riding stables and gave the palace a new façade. The apartments were decorated in the Rocaille style by Germain Boffrand in the 1730s. Attached to the National Archives, the Hôtel de Soubise houses the Museum of French History.
60, Rue des Francs-Bourgeois (3rd)

The **Hôtel de Sully**, built starting in 1625, belongs to the late Renaissance style, as evidenced by the great sloping roofs, ornate dormer windows, and relief decoration on the façades. Its name remains connected to that of King Henry IV's famous superintendent of finances, who acquired it in 1634. His descendants expanded the residence over the course of the 17th century, adding a garden wing. State property since 1944, the Hôtel de Sully houses the headquarters of the Center for National Monuments.

62, Rue Saint-Antoine (4th)

HOTEL DE SULLY

Place des Vosges

(3th and 4th arrondissements)

This royal square was created on the site of the former Hôtel des Tournelles where King Henry II died in 1559 from injuries sustained in a tournament. Catherine de' Medici razed the building in which her husband had lain dying for 10 days; she moved to the Louvre. The cleared land was taken over by a horse market, then by a "Court of Miracles" (a place where beggars lived and shed their feigned afflictions after their day's work). Henry IV set up a silk factory here in 1604 and wanted to complement it with a square surrounded on three other sides by housing suitable for the workers. The concessions were granted to private investors on the condition they build according to a unique, pre-established plan, using the same materials: brick, stone, and slate. The factory quickly went under and was razed in 1607. In its stead, houses were built to resemble those on the other sides of the square.
The Place Royale was inaugurated by Louis XIII in 1612, on the occasion of his marriage to Anne of Austria. It became an aristocratic and sought-after address until the 19th century.
Place Royale changed its name several times; it became Place des Vosges in 1800 to honor the fiscal virtue of the department whose inhabitants had been the first to pay their taxes.

Place de la Bastille

(4th, 11th, and 12th arrondissements)

Very different from the skillfully designed model of royal squares, Place de la Bastille developed more freely and is more like a crossroads. At the start of Rue Saint-Antoine, the main thoroughfare of Paris under the Ancien Régime, the Bastille was the cradle of the revolutions, starting with the one in 1789. On July 14 of that year, the crowd took the famous fortress, the symbol of royal absolutism.
There is almost nothing left of the Bastille prison whose past presence is only indicated with a paved outline on the ground.
The revolution of 1830 left a more visible reminder – the bronze column engraved with the names of the victims of the July insurrection.
To these were added the names of those who died in the revolution of 1848.
The "July column" is capped with the gilded bronze statue of the "Spirit of Freedom".
The Bastille Opera was built by Carlos Ott on the site of the former Bastille train station as part of the major municipal construction projects of the 1980s. It was inaugurated for the bicentennial of the Revolution.
Unlike the Palais Garnier, this new "people's" opera was meant to slip into the existing urban fabric without altering an entire neighborhood.
That is indeed what the Bastille Opera achieved, standing along one whole side of the Place and stretching back along Rue de Lyon. However, its heavy, shapeless architecture only shows its personality after nightfall, thanks to the lighting by Yann Kersalé.

La Villette

Between Avenue Corentin-Cariou
and Avenue Jean-Jaurès (19th)

The Cité des sciences et de l'industrie (City of Science and Industry) is located in the vast auction building of the former La Villette abattoirs, a gargantuan machine which went bankrupt almost before it was put into service.
250 meters long and 110 meters wide, the building has seven storeys and houses a permanent exhibition as well as temporary events to aid a quality popularization of science.
The vast park is dotted with red buildings, the "follies" imagined by architect Bernard Tschumi. It also boasts the Géode, a sphere 36 meters in diameter, inside of which there is a hemispherical movie theater that plunges viewers into the image. There is also the Cité de la musique (City of Music), a conservatory and museum built by Christian de Portzamparc, the Zénith, a major concert hall inaugurated in 1984 and intended to exist for only three years, but whose success gave it greater longevity…
In this ensemble, the most venerable element is the Grande Halle built in 1867 for the first livestock market in La Villette. Today, it hosts performances and events.

Sacré-Cœur Basilica

Parvis du Sacré-Cœur (18th)

In 1870, a few pious intellectuals moved by the recent demise of the Papal States wanted to affirm the vigor of Christianity in the face of the secular ideals upheld by the representatives of the new republic. They launched a popular subscription in order to build a basilica to the Sacred Heart of Jesus at the top of Montmartre hill – reputed site of the martyrdom of Saint Denis. This highly controversial project was nonetheless passed by parliamentarians, and work began in 1876. It continued for over 40 years, because the ground on the butte, unstable and riddled with quarries, meant that very deep wells had to be dug to provide the foundations of the structure.

Altered and modified many times, the plans for Sacré-Cœur attest to the 19th-century taste for eclecticism. The monument features the Romanesque tradition of semicircular arches, as well as Byzantine colors in the cascade of cupolas freely inspired by the Hagia Sophia in Constantinople. Additionally, the stone used to build it is unusual in that it whitens in contact with rain, which further accentuates the building's strangeness in the urban landscape. Nestled in the bell tower near the apse, there is the nineteen-ton "Savoyarde", the heaviest bell in Paris. The basilica was consecrated in October, 1919. It has become a draw for pilgrims as well as tourists, its omnipresence in the Parisian skyline having made it a potent symbol.

François Mitterrand National Library of France

11, Quai François-Mauriac (13th)

The new library on the banks of the Seine was created due to the congestion of its elder sister in Rue de Richelieu. Its aims were loftier than simply providing more stacks, because it was meant to be open to new information technology. In 1989, French President François Mitterrand chose the project by Dominique Perrault, which planned for a hollowed-out base to house a garden and four high corner towers, to represent open books. Each tower has seven floors of offices, while eleven others are devoted to storing works. This approach of conserving books above ground, albeit behind wooden shutters to protect them from the sun, and having the lecture halls below ground sparked much criticism while the project was under development and when the new library was put into service.

The fact remains that the François Mitterrand Library has increased the capacity of the former National Library six-fold, and it holds thirteen million books and other printed matter.

It also possesses one of the oldest manuscripts in the world, the Prisse papyrus (circa – 1,900 B.C.E.)

BnF
T3

National Museum of Natural History and The Medicinal Garden

57, Rue Cuvier and 2, Place Valhubert (5th)

In 1626, under Louis XIII, the royal medicinal garden was created, but it was Buffon, in the 18th century, who gave it its true character, turning the simple garden run by the King's physician into a research center that attracted the great naturalists.
The oldest gallery of the Museum is the one devoted to mineralogy, built between 1833 and 1841.
Built in 1889, like the Eiffel Tower, the glass-roofed zoology gallery was meant to house over one million specimens. The gallery was poorly maintained and fell into such disrepair that it was closed to the public in 1965. It was given a zinc roof in 1968 to stop the rain streaming through the broken windows and damaging the collections. A long night fell on the grand gallery, whose doors remained closed. Its resurrection only came in 1994, after a massive State renovation led by the architects Chemetov and Huidobro, which gave rise to the spectacular Grand Gallery of Evolution, whose three levels of scenography present the diversity of living things, the evolution of life, and man's role in evolution.

Arab World Institute

1, Rue des Fossés-Saint-Bernard (5th)

Inaugurated in 1987, the Arab World Institute, the fruit of a partnership between France and twenty-two Arab countries, is a museum, a multi-media center, and a library. On the banks of the Seine, on the edge of historical Paris, the building designed by the teams of Jean Nouvel and Architecture Studio had to be in harmony with its environment and represent a dialogue of cultures. On the Seine side, glass and steel face the stone of Old Paris just as the prow of the building – which brings to mind a narrow medina street – looks towards the apse of Notre-Dame. The most spectacular façade gives onto the forecourt, composed of large panels fitted with motor-controlled apertures shaped like moucharabieh windows, filtering more or less light, depending on the brightness of the day.
Inside, futuristic transparent elevators whisk visitors up to the roof terrace. It provides a breathtaking view of the Île Saint-Louis and the Île de la Cité.

Val-de-Grâce

1, Place Alphonse-Laveran (5th)

The construction of the church of Val-de-Grâce fulfilled Anne of Austria's wish. She had promised to dedicate "a magnificent temple to God" if he granted her the son she had not yet managed to bear. The birth of the future King Louis XIV gave rise to this grandiose church, to which were added a monastery and a residence for the queen. It was the young king, then seven years old, who laid the first stone in 1645. François Mansart, very inspired by Italian Baroque, was not able to complete the structure for which he had drawn the plans.
The preliminary reinforcements which were necessary because the ground was riddled with former mines consumed almost the entire budget meant for construction. In 1646 the buildings controller deemed it more prudent to replace the spendthrift architect with Jacques Lemercier. Other architects completed the work in 1667.
The interior decor of the church's dome is extremely rich. A spectacular canopy, inspired by the one in St. Peter's in Rome, is supported by six twisted columns. On the floor, the colors and delicacy of the marble marquetry rival the cupola's fresco.
A passageway from the Saint-Louis chapel leads to the cloisters, now occupied by military health services. In 1793, the convent of Val-de-Grâce was turned into a military hospital. It remains one today.

Panthéon

Place du Panthéon (5th)

Louis XV had ordered the architect Soufflot to build a church at the top of the Montagne Sainte –Geneviève. The first stone was laid in 1764. Its style marks a return to classical tastes; this is particularly evident in the columns. Its overall design is quite similar to the Invalides church: a triple dome caps the building, which is constructed on a Greek-cross-shaped floor plan.
Dedicated to Saint Geneviève, patron saint of Parisians, the monument's function changed under the Revolution, becoming the national necropolis for great men.
The walls, once pierced with windows, were blocked up to create darkness in keeping with the reverential atmosphere of a "national Pantheon". The outlines of certain windows remain visible from the outside.
Several times, as the regimes of the 19th century evolved, the building was devoted to worship, then to a new pantheon. It was only in 1885, on the occasion of Victor Hugo's funeral, that it finally became a place of interment and memory. More than sixty bodies rest in the crypt, including two women: Sophie Berthelot and Marie Curie. The simplicity and similarity of the tombs seem to express sobriety and equality in death.
It was under the dome of the Pantheon in 1851 that Foucault's pendulum experiment proved that the Earth revolved.

National Museum of the Middle Ages – Cluny Baths

6, Place Paul-Painlevé (5th)

A rare example of medieval secular architecture in Paris, this town house was built at the end of the 15th century for the abbots of Cluny on the initiative of Jacques d'Amboise, an important Church dignitary and brother of Cardinal Georges d'Amboise, the king's first minister. The building was a forerunner the model of the "hôtel particulier", between courtyard and garden, which was to have great success in the following centuries. Here, two uneven wings extend from the main building to define a nearly triangular courtyard, closed off from Rue Du Sommerard by a crenellated wall. Intricate sculpted decoration adorns the balustrade, the dormer windows, and the tower. This house was hardly used by the abbots but welcomed foreign sovereigns on several occasions. Cardinal Mazarin resided here in 1634. Vandalized during the Revolution, the building was then occupied by various artisans who continued to degrade it for the requirements of their activities. Restored and connected to the neighboring Gallo-Roman baths, the structure was turned into a medieval museum in 1843. Its first displays were already composed of the collections of the erudite Alexandre Du Sommerard, who was passionate about medieval artifacts and who had moved into the Hôtel de Cluny to live and to allow enthusiasts to view his treasures there.

Luxembourg Palace – The Senate

15, Rue de Vaugirard (6th)

The Luxembourg Palace was built starting in 1615 by Salomon de Brosse for Marie de' Medici.
The queen wanted a residence that would remind her of her Florentine childhood, and the Italianate bossages of the Luxembourg have often been compared to those of the Palazzo Pitti.
The queen wanted the decoration to be sumptuous – she commissioned no fewer than 24 paintings from Rubens to adorn her gallery – and the work lasted fifteen years. Forced into exile, Marie de' Medici only enjoyed her residence very briefly.
The palace had other illustrious occupants: the Duchess de Guise, Madame de Maintenon and the children of Louis XIV, the Duchess de Berry, and the Count of Provence…
The Revolution turned it into a prison and the First Empire set up the Senate there. In 1835, the Luxembourg Palace underwent major expansion work which led to the construction of a new façade on the garden, imitating the original composition.
The palace remains the seat the Senate. With their many statues, the gardens are thought to be the most beautiful in Paris. The terraces, vistas, and flowerbed compositions make it a remarkable example of a French garden, except in the more sinuous southwestern part.

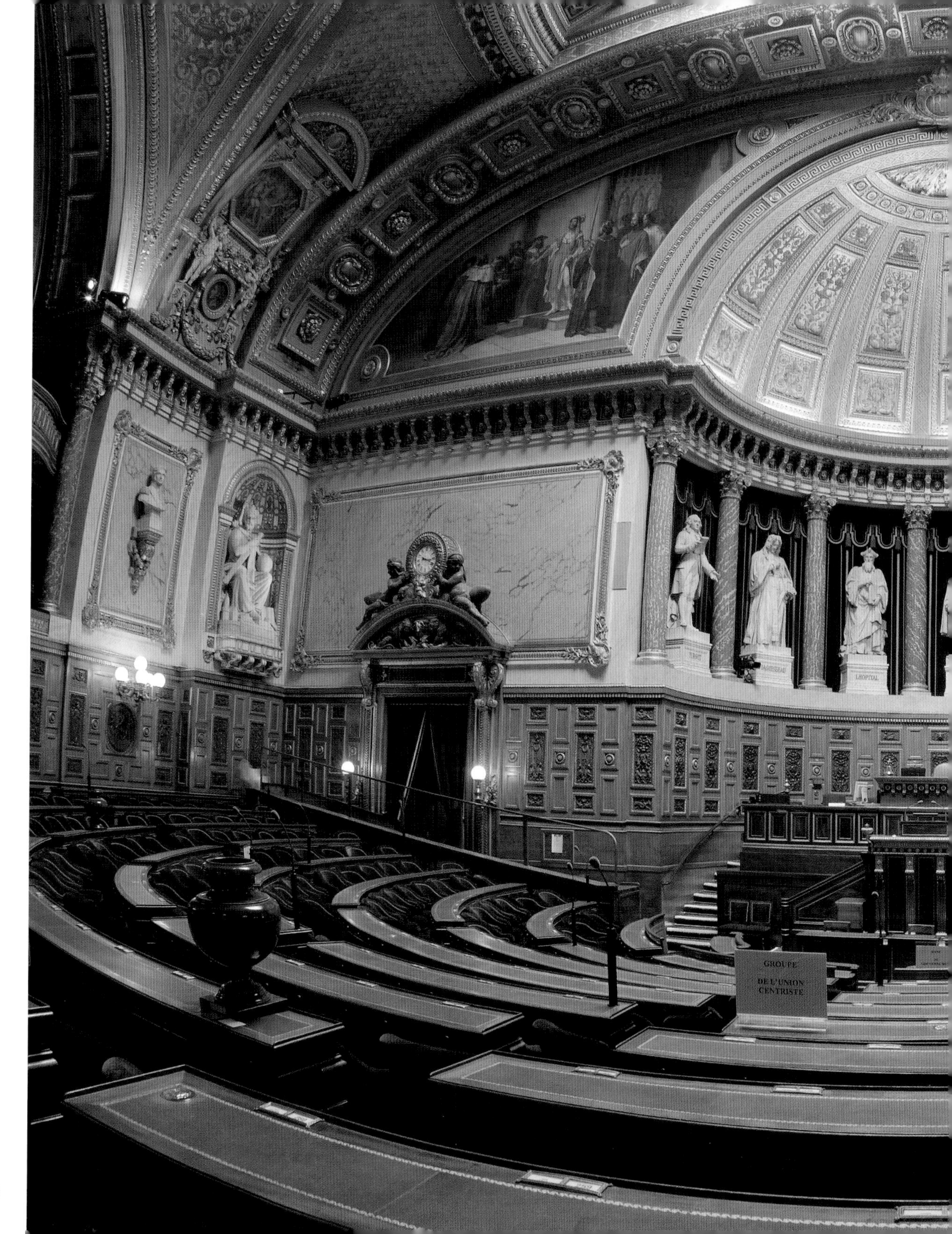
GROUPE
DE L'UNION
CENTRISTE

Hôtel de la Monnaie (Paris Mint)

2, Rue Guénégaud (6th)

A factory installed in a palace! One of the most imposing buildings on the banks of the Seine was indeed used for minting coins, a kingly activity since the 9th century. Completed in 1775, the Hôtel de la Monnaie was the last Parisian monument created during the reign of Louis XV. It is also the most sober. Its long straight façade parallel to the river is only enlivened by a central avant-corps with classical columns topped with six statues personifying virtues. The rigor of this neoclassical architecture, so in vogue at the end of the 18th century, is in sharp contrast to the roundness of the headquarters of the Institute of France built one hundred years earlier next to the Monnaie.
In 1973, coin striking moved to the Pessac workshops in the Gironde. Only medal designs and coin dies were kept at the Parisian mint. It also houses a numismatic museum.

Institute of France

23, Quai Conti (6th)

The lucky academics who work here do so in one of the most beautiful buildings attributed to a public organization! Since its creation in 1795, it has been the Institute of France's mission to promote arts and sciences through five academies. The most prestigious, and the oldest, is the Académie Française, founded in 1635. Its forty members, dubbed "Immortals" and elected by their peers, are guardians of the French language. They guarantee proper usage and ratify its evolutions in a patiently developed dictionary.
The publication of the ninth edition began in 1992.
Since 1805, the seat of the Institute has been in the former College of the Four Nations. It was built between 1662 and 1688, as set out in the will of Cardinal and Minister Mazarin, for the education of sixty gentlemen from four provinces recently annexed by France. The architect Le Vau drew up the plans. This was his most Italianate work. The dome of the chapel and the semicircular wings recall the St. Peter's Basilica and Square in Rome. The ultramontane influence is also visible in the pronounced use of rounded lines. They contrast with the austerity of the south wing of the Cour Carrée of the Louvre on the other side of the Seine, also designed by Le Vau.

SVB VMBRACVLO

IN MEDIO

Musée d'Orsay

1, Rue de la Légion-d'Honneur (7th)

In 1900, as Paris was holding the Universal Exhibition, the Orléans Railway Company was inaugurating its Parisian terminus on the Quai d'Orsay on the banks of the Seine. Architect Victor Laloux covered the metallic structure of this prestigious train station with stone façades, the better to have it blend into its environment and not impose an industrial-looking neighbor on the Louvre on the other bank. On the Seine side, statues representing the cities served nevertheless to recall the building's function.

Poorly adapted to growing traffic, the station was almost completely abandoned in 1939. For a long time, the building had no purpose and was threatened with destruction before the idea to turn it into a great Parisian museum devoted to the art of the second half of the 19th century, and particularly to Impressionism.

The renovation work was conducted between 1981 and 1986. Tasked with the interior renovations, Italian architect Gae Aulenti preserved the luxurious reception rooms of the station's former hotel as well as the glass and metal vault above the great nave. The space is vast and luminous while leaving the initial function of the building apparent. The Musée d'Orsay was inaugurated in December 1986, forming its collections from those of the Louvre, the Jeu de Paume museum, and the National Modern Art Museum.

GYMKHANA
GYMKHANA 1

Musée d'Orsay
Musée d'Orsay

ASSEMBLEE NATIONALE

National Assembly

33, Quai d'Orsay (7th)

This palace, built between 1722 and 1728, began as that of the Duchess de Bourbon, daughter of Louis XIV and Madame de Montespan. It was expanded on the eve of the Revolution by the Prince of Condé, who added two wings on the main courtyard. However, it was under the Empire that a new façade was superimposed on the Seine side of the Palais-Bourbon.
This neoclassical peristyle echoes its twin on the Madeleine Church in the view across Place de la Concorde and along Rue Royale.
Housing the legislative body of the Council of Five Hundred during the Revolution, the Palace then became the seat of the Chamber of Deputies, which became the National Assembly in 1946.
Inside, the "semicircle" or the session chamber, on the site of the Duchess de Bourbon's former reception rooms, houses the 577 members of parliament from around the country. Elected directly by universal suffrage every five years, their role is to pass laws, to monitor government actions, and to evaluate public policies.
The Assembly has a very rich library that includes 600,000 works, some of which are rare manuscripts. This great gallery is capped with remarkable cupolas painted by Eugène Delacroix.

Invalides

129, Rue de Grenelle (7th)

It was on Louis XIV's initiative that the Hôtel des Invalides was created to take in wounded soldiers or those too old to serve. Previously, these military men had to rely on the benevolence of monasteries, when they weren't reduced to begging.
Vast buildings were constructed outside the city, accommodating just over one thousand residents shortly after the inauguration in 1674. Soon, their numbers increased to over 4,000. The establishment included dormitories, refectories, an infirmary.... On the south side of the main courtyard, surrounded by arcades, stands the entrance to the church of Saint-Louis des Invalides, known as the Soldiers' Church.
Flags taken from the enemy are on exhibit in its nave.
Adjacent to this first church, the Church of the Dome was built by Jules Hardouin-Mansart for the king, who had his very own entrance fit for his station. It is capped with a spectacular dome whose gilding lights up with the first rays of sunlight.
The Church of the Dome has become a military necropolis, housing several tombs, the most famous of which is the red quartzite tomb of Napoleon, set in a rotunda which was created in the center of the building in the 1850s.

Alexander III Bridge

Between Quai d'Orsay (7th)
and Cours de La Reine (8th)

We owe the most beautiful bridge in Paris to the Universal Exhibition of 1900. Its allegorical figures, classical columns, and sculpted flowers echo the decor of the Grand Palais and the Petit Palais, located nearby and built at the same time. All three work together to create a prestigious view between Invalides and the Champs-Élysées.
Under its opulent decoration, the bridge reveals great technical qualities: the roadway is lowered and is not made up of two slightly inclined pieces, as most bridges were at the time.
These characteristics meant no obstacle was created to the view of the façade of the Invalides. To facilitate river traffic, it is composed of just one arch, a feature made possible through the use of steel, a material still rarely used at the time for structural work. Additionally, reinforced abutments topped with tall counterweight pillars were installed on the embankments.
While the Alexander III Bridge is the most ornate in Paris, it is also full of political meaning: named in honor of the Russian Tsar who signed an important alliance with France in 1893, it is a link between the two countries, bearing as it does the coat of arms of the Seine and Paris on the west and that of the Neva and Russia on the other.

Quai Branly Museum

37, Quai Branly (7th)

The most recent of the great Parisian museums, the Quai Branly Museum was inaugurated in 2006 by French President Jacques Chirac, who was also behind the project. It is devoted to the indigenous arts of the civilizations of Africa, Oceania, Asia, and the Americas. Jean Nouvel created the buildings for the new institution. The main building is shaped like a metal bridge – the Eiffel Tower is nearby – to which are attached colored boxes. It is surrounded by a garden designed by landscape architect Gilles Clément.
Inside, a long ramp leads to the main gallery, which is dimly lit so as not to damage the sunlight-sensitive pieces. Giving directly onto the quay, the administration building is remarkable for its immense and spectacular garden wall, designed by Patrick Blanc, which serves as its façade.

Eiffel Tower

Champ-de-Mars (7th)

On the occasion of the Universal Exhibition of 1889, the fledgling Third Republic intended to fly the French colors high. Eiffel the engineer took up this challenge, planning to build a 30-meter-high tower. It took him and 300 workers just 26 months to assemble what he called "the biggest flagpole in the world". The tower is a technical feat but also a masterpiece of metallic architecture. The main function of the arches under the first floor is to insert themselves into the play of straight lines. The bundle shape of the tower accentuates its slenderness, and the openwork iron gives it great finesse as well as great lightness. Furthermore, the Eiffel Tower only weighs 7,000 tons.

For forty years, the Tower was the tallest construction in the world. It remains the symbol of upward expansion, precursor to the dawn of aviation. This emblem of Paris and of all of France was meant to be dismantled twenty years after its completion. But Eiffel's outspokenness, public approval of the monument, and its role in the development of radio saved it.

Since 2003, the lighting set up for the New Year's celebrations of 2000 has once again been activated, and the tower sparkles each hour on the hour after nightfall.

Saint-Denis Basilica

1, Rue de la Légion-d'Honneur,
Saint-Denis (93)

The tall silhouette of Saint-Denis Basilica stands just outside Paris. It was built starting in the 12th century on the site of successive sanctuaries which stood where Saint Denis is supposed to have fallen after having suffered his martyrdom in Montmartre.
The renown of the saint, the first evangelist in Paris, made this basilica the necropolis for the kings of France. Dagobert was buried there in 639, and starting with the death of Hugues Capet in 996, practically all the sovereigns, with very few exceptions, were interred in the church, then in the current basilica. The choir was built in 1144. Featuring ribbed vaults and large stained-glass windows, elements which were novel at the time, it is seen as the first major Gothic construction.
In 1793, the tombs were desecrated, and the adjoining abbey's treasury suffered great losses. Major restoration work was carried out in the 19th century. It was completed with the intervention of Viollet-le-Duc from 1846 to 1879, saving the building from ruin and arranging the tombs in the manner we see today.

Statues of Louis XVI and Marie-Antoinette.

Recumbent effigy of Clovis.

LEROY MERLIN
Centre de Recherche

Prayers of a different nature sometimes rise heavenward from another building in Saint-Denis. The **Stade de France** was built in record time for the soccer World Cup in 1998. The 80,000-seat stadium hosts major sporting events as well as concerts and other performances.

Grand Arch of La Défense, La Défense district

Paris-La Défense (92)

In the mid-1950s, a decision was made to create the modern business district Paris lacked and could not create within its walls. A zone that straddled three municipalities, disadvantaged but located in the continuation of the Champs-Élysées, was made viable, built up, and connected to the road and rail networks. La Défense, virtually the 21st arrondissement of Paris, got its name from a bronze statue commemorating the defense of Paris during the siege of the war of 1870. The statue was installed in 1883 at the traffic circle in Courbevoie, now the entrance to the business district. Since 1958, the year the massive concrete vault of the CNIT (National Center for Industries and Techniques) was constructed, several dozen office towers have been built in La Défense, giving an overview of the changes in architecture over the last half century. The Arch was inaugurated in 1989. A 110-meter-high concrete cube covered in white Carrera marble, the monument is meant to be "an open window to the world", according to its Danish designer, Otto von Spreckelsen. The structure is amazing large; you could fit Notre-Dame cathedral and its spire under the Arch! It also constitutes the third landmark in the historical perspective of Paris, after the Arc du Carrousel and the Arc de Triomphe.

AREVA
Cœur Défense

Palace of Versailles

Place d'Armes, Versailles (78)

Versailles was nothing but a humble hunting lodge built in 1623 for the king's use; it sheltered Louis XIV's first amorous adventures with Mademoiselle de la Vallière. The memory of those happy days and conversely those of the torments of the Fronde in Paris inspired the king to expand and beautify the domain in 1662. Depending on available resources and during peaceful periods, the works created great momentum. Tens of thousands of workers took part, marble quarries were dug, long canals and imposing aqueducts had to be created to supply the gardens and fountains with water, and newly established factories produced countless items of furniture and decoration.

In 1682, Versailles was already fully participating in the glorification of the Sun King when he decided to set up permanent residence and the government there. More construction projects followed. Jules Hardouin-Mansart transformed the central terrace into the Hall of Mirrors in which solid silver furniture was displayed. Apartments occupied two new wings and a vast chapel marked the end of construction work in 1710. Louis XV added to his great-grandfather's work by constructing an opera house.

The Hall of Mirrors.

The Opera.

The Chapel.

The Queen's Hamlet with the Marlborough Tower.

The French Pavilion at the Trianon.

The Latona Fountain during the "nocturnal fountain show".

Some practical advice for photographing Paris

Paris is the world's anywhere leading tourist destination, the most visited and photographed city in the world. With the digital revolution of the last decade, thousands of images of Paris are taken each day, by amateurs and professionals alike. This short chapter aims is to give readers tips on how to achieve better photographs, whether they're Parisians or tourists on their first visit.

Planning ahead to be in the right place at the right time

The most important aspect of photography is light. The most wonderful subject in bad light will not make for a good photograph. This is especially important for daytime photography using natural light. All the images in this book were taken when the light was optimum. This means that some images are better created at certain time of the year, depending on the position of the sun in the sky as well as the geographic position of the monuments you are trying to photograph. Weather forecasting is of great importance. High-pressure systems make for stable and sunny weather, whereas low-pressure systems make for more dramatic but less predictable light. Accurate weather forecasts and astronomical data (ephemerides of the sun and moon) are easy to find on the Internet. Put simply, predicting the best time to take a photograph will make your images much stronger.

Composition, or expressing a personal vision

"Composition is the strongest way of seeing" – Edward Weston. Composition is one of the most important aspects of photography. Its aim is to express your vision and your emotional response to the scene. We recommend you start by using the traditional rules of composition (Rule of Thirds, Golden Rule, leading lines, diagonals…). Give equal importance to all the areas of the frame. You should start by studying and learning to master these rules. When you have done so, you can start breaking the rules to create your own compositions. Take the time to walk the scene and previsualize your images. Try to create both horizontal and vertical compositions. The ultimate goal of composition is the development of a personal style, not to recreate what other photographers have done before.

A few technical considerations

Although most modern digital cameras give good results using the various automatic modes, the best results will be obtained by learning to use your camera in manual mode. For each image, use the best combination of the three variables of photography (aperture, shutter speed, ISO). Use only the aperture necessary to obtain the desired depth of field. Using an unnecessarily small aperture (f22) will result in diffraction and a softer image. To get optimum data, use the raw file format (DSLR or advanced compact cameras only). Use the histogram function to check for highlights and shadows. Get the sharpest images by determining the optimum aperture for each of your lenses.

Canon 5D Mark II, Canon 70-200/f4 L IS, ISO 100, f/11, 15s, ND4 filter.

Canon 20D, Canon 70-200/f4 L IS. 3 HDR images (bracketing: -2/0/+2) created with Photomatix Pro then assembled as a panorama with Autopano Pro.

Night photography, a perilous undertaking

Night photography is one of the most challenging aspects of photography. Even with recent technological advances like image stabilization and low-noise high-ISO images, there is no substitute for a sturdy tripod. Buy the best tripod you can. The best light is usually obtained about 30 minutes after sunset. Use a remote control or the self-timer to avoid camera shake. Use mirror lock-up, especially with telephoto lenses. If conditions are windy, increase the ISO to get a shorter exposure time. Because at night the only sources of light are artificial lights (tungsten, neon lights), which have a different color temperature than direct sunlight, we do not recommend using automatic white balance. Either use the night scene modes (compact cameras) or set the color temperature manually (DSLR cameras), and check the LCD screen and the histogram. If shooting in raw format, you can adjust the color temperature in the raw converter. It can be interesting to use long exposures (5s up to 30s) when photographing some night scenes (to get light streaks from car traffic, or to get a smooth water surface). To do this, you need a neutral density filter (ND4, ND8) that will reduce the amount of light reaching the sensor without changing the color balance.

Taking better advantage of HDR technology

HDR technology, the combination of several photographs of the same scene at different exposure levels, is particularly useful when shooting night scenes or interiors. It should be used when obtaining detailed information both in the highlights and shadows in one exposure is impossible. This technique is best done using a tripod and the bracketing mode found in most advanced compact cameras and DSLRs. There should be no moving elements in the scene you're photographing (cars, pedestrians, animals). You have to use manual mode, as the aperture and ISO settings must not change during the different exposures. Special software such as Photomatix Pro or Photoshop can then be used to combine the exposures and create the final image. When shooting scenes with sufficient light levels, you can make the different exposures without a tripod as long as the slowest exposure does not result in a blurred image due to camera shake.

Panoramic photography

One advantage of digital photography is the easy creation of panoramic images by combining several photographs. These images are wider-angle, more detailed, and less distorted than can be easily produced with a single photograph. Take all images in manual mode at the same settings. Use a tripod with a level base and overlap the pictures by at least 20%. Use a panoramic head to avoid parallax error if shooting a scene with a close foreground. During the daytime, you can shoot handheld as long as the subject photographed is far enough away to avoid parallax errors. If shooting in raw, convert all the raw files with the same settings and color balance. Assemble the images with software such as Autopano Pro, Panorama Tool or Photoshop or the application provided by your camera's manufacturer. It should be noted than the HDR and panoramic techniques can be combined together. In this case, the HDR images should be prepared first and then assembled in a second step.

The importance of postproduction

Postproduction is the stage in which you make the final adjustments to the image and optimize it. It is an integral part of the photographic process. Convert your raw files by adjusting parameters such as color balance, contrast, and saturation. It is not necessary to do all the optimization work in the raw converter. More advanced users should optimize their photographs using layers in a photo-editing software (Photoshop Elements, PaintShop Pro, GIMP). Save the final images in a lossless file format (TIFF, PSD). Don't forget to back up your images (DVDs, hard drives, online back-up).

Technical notes

Arnaud Chicurel used a Nikon D300 with Nikon and Sigma lenses (Sigma 10/f2.8, Nikkor 12-24/f4 DX, 24-70/f2.8, 80-200/f2.8).
Pascal Ducept used a Canon 5D MkII and Canon EF lenses (15/f2.8, 17-40/f4 L, 24-70/f2.8 L, 50/f1.4, 70-200/f4 L IS and 400/f5.6 L).

Arnaud Chicurel is a lecturer at the Louvre Museum and the Center for National Monuments. He is also a professional photographer whose images are regularly published in the press. He likes taking pictures of Paris and also enjoys aerial and underwater photography. He has written books on the Red Sea.
E-mail: arnchicurel@yahoo.fr

Pascal Ducept has a Ph.D. in chemistry and has worked as a researcher at Colorado State University. His trips through the Rockies and U.S. national parks sparked his passion for photography. Since returning to France in 2005, he has devoted himself full-time to this art, particularly to taking pictures of Paris.
E-mail: pducept@gmail.com

Images by Arnaud Chicurel and Pascal Ducept are distributed through the Hemis agency (www.hemis.fr).

Edition: Mathilde Kressmann and Margot Rietsch

Art direction: Isabelle Chemin

Printed in France by Mame (Tours)

Dépôt légal : juin 2011
ISBN: 978-2-84096-728-6